M.

BEFORE YOU STAND

A PRACTICAL GUIDE TO WORSHIP MINISTRY

FOREWORD BY PASTOR DAVID R. BRINSON

Bless You!

MP

MONTEL POWERS

Published by:
Ellis & Ellis Consulting Group, LLC
www.ellisandellisconsulting.org
678-438-3574/242-347-2347

ISBN 13: 978-1508481911
10: 1508481911

Printed in the United States of America.

DEDICATION

To Pastor Teddy Parker Jr.

When I was 11 years old you obeyed God and gave me the opportunity to serve. You taught me how to be a true, faithful servant. Without your sensitivity to the Spirit of God I would not be where I am today. You took a chance on a young kid that had a gift and a desire to be used by God and I will forever HONOR you for that. I love and miss you!

Trecie, Kamry, and Kerrington his legacy lives on through you and every life that he touched directly as well as indirectly. WHAT A LEGACY! Love you!

Montel Powers

CONTENTS

FOREWORD

In life, often we are offered opportunities of a lifetime; some may seize upon them, and others take them for granted. In my short lifetime, I have had the privilege to serve as worship pastor and minister of music for a number of God's generals. With every assignment, God sent people ready to help fulfill the vision and call of the worship ministry. There was never a shortage of singers and musicians to meet the musical and vocal demands in ministry; however, missing was the opportunity to pour into sons and daughters who would be receptive to aligning with principles of worship, and then came Montel Powers.

Montel came to me looking for a mentor years ago, and God allowed me to guide him as a father in ministry into a healthy place, both mentally and spiritually. His hunger and quest to embrace worship with a pure heart caused my spirit to leap! The experience was likened to the feeling you get during the birthing and rearing processes, similar to fathering my own biological children, but this was a spiritual act and process.

With Montel's thirst and yearning to learn worship, as I knew it, I believe, it has triggered his desire to share his understanding of the worship experience with the world. Musically, Montel gets it; Spiritually, Montel gets it - His ear for the sound of worship (God and the flow of worship) is impeccable. He is a man of honor, integrity, prayer, and accountability, and now he wants to share his heart with worship and ministry leaders all over the world in his new book.

This book will not only give you a little insight on who Montel Powers is as a man of God, worship leader, and Christian, but also provide a glimpse of the supernatural revelation and impartation received from just listening, watching, serving, and walking it out, while making adjustments along the way. I pray as you read and study this book, the principles on the pages would become a lifestyle for you and not just another book you read, and that you become a living example for generations to come.

David R. Brinson
Senior Pastor
Eighth Day Church, Inc.
Warner Robins, Georgia

CHAPTER ONE

What Can I Expect from this Book?

As believers we were given the most honorable position of all time. God created us to worship, His son and our Lord and Savior, Jesus Christ. No matter what our particular assignments are, as it relates to ministry, we all have this mandate in common. The very lives that we live are to be lived in a way that honors and pleases God, which is an act of worship. But we know that there is a time in our weekly gatherings where we join together to corporately worship God through song. As I said before, it is an honor to be chosen to worship Him but I believe that it's an even greater honor to be graced with the anointing to lead people in this capacity.

The Worship Leader leads the corporate body to a place where our hearts are open to receive the preached (spoken) word of God. When the word is released it can now take root in, and penetrate our hearts so that we are prompted to change. As you can imagine this obviously means that the role of the Worship Leader in your church is extremely important. We have often lacked education and proper knowledge in this area of ministry, which has led to frustration and burn out for so many people that have this assignment. The scripture states in the fourth chapter of Hosea that, "My people perish for a lack of knowledge." It has never been and will never be the Will of God for any of us to become weary and abort the call that He has placed on our lives. It's vital that there is an awareness and sensitivity to be diligent and accurate concerning your assignment, to prevent these things from happening.

Contrary to what some of us may believe there is a way to walk this out effectively without being consistently frustrated. We have accepted some things and quote sayings such as, "I guess this is just how it is." This is inaccurate. It is also not the Will of God for you to remain in a place of frustration. The problem that we often run into when God allows us to enter those seasons of temporary frustration is we prolong those seasons because we fail to follow instructions. Again, this most likely happens because of one of two reasons, either we don't have knowledge on what to do or we have the knowledge and choose to disobey. In case you were wondering let me clarify something now so that we are on the same page, partially obeying God is the same as disobeying Him. He intends for us to pray and seek Him so that we can learn exactly what He desires for us to learn and be released. Once we have applied what we've learned we are now able to elevate past that particular place. Many times we search for answers from things and people that don't have the ability to help us. Our deliverance is delayed because we are trying to pull from the wrong source. When we take those cares directly to God, He is faithful to answer every question and bring clarity to all uncertainties. The choice is totally ours so I want you to authoritatively speak this declaration out of your mouth right now with me: *"I choose not to operate out of frustration in my assignment of leading worship."* Say it with power and conviction causing it to matriculate to the core of who you are as *HIS* worship leader.

I HAVE QUESTIONS

So many different questions may come to mind when you hear the term "Worship Leader" and think about the overall description of the title.

Here are a few:

- What are the requirements to walk and operate as a Worship Leader?

- How do I enhance my sensitivity to be able to flow during worship?

- How do I know how to navigate in the midst of the worship service?

- How do I get my team to understand the importance of the assignment?

- How should I conduct my rehearsals?

- How do I make sure that we all remain on the same page?

These are all questions that every worship leader has either previously asked, or is currently asking. Self-evaluation is a great thing for

> *"I choose not to operate out of frustration in my assignment of leading worship."*

the lead worshipper to do on a consistent basis to make sure YOU aren't standing in the way of what God is doing. Leading worship is often viewed as a glamorous position. After all you get to stand before people on a weekly basis and use your gift to glorify God. Everyone knows who you are and loves you and loves the way you do what you do. Should be a pretty easy task as long as you learn the music and come prepared, right? WRONG! Let me help you by saying if this is your idea of leading worship, then this is definitely the book for you, because those things have absolutely nothing to do with the call. Now don't get me wrong, these things come with the territory but should never become a focal point for the Worship Leader. This calling is so much more than that.

We have made these misconceptions without having true knowledge of what this office really entails. It is an assignment that you can't call yourself to, but it is also an assignment that you can't avoid when you've truly been called. Depending on your denominational background or demographic location you may have used the term Worship Leader but may not have gained a true understanding of who this person is. In my years of ministry I have also been able to see that there are many discrepancies about the responsibilities for the Worship Leader/ Worship Pastor. There are a number of things that are prerequisites before the worship leader sets foot on the platform. I received a mandate from God to educate and empower people to walk into their purpose with knowledge and wisdom, thus the reason you are able to read this book.

I believe, as leaders, we are to teach and impart into those around us so that they can receive truth, which will then have the power to become revelation to them. Once it becomes revelation we have the amazing opportunity to change the way that we've always done things because now we are functioning from a place of TRUTH. We can be delivered from what we previously thought and now function from a place of what we KNOW. The truth is what frees us. You can be free to flow right into your rightful position in the Kingdom as a Worship Leader of the only true and Living God. So I'm sure by now you are wondering, *"So what does it actually take to be an effective worship leader?"* Throughout this book you will see that there are many things that take place before the Worship Leader even stands before God's people.

<u>CHAPTER TWO</u>

THE FOUNDATION
Prayer, Fasting and Intercession

Sneak Peek: In this chapter we will discuss the foundation for anyone that desires to serve/ lead in ministry. We will pin point tools and key principles that God has directed us to live by. These tools will give insight and sustain you through the great and challenging times on this journey of leading the corporate body in worship.

My Personal Relationship with God Matters

When I first started leading worship I adopted the idea that music was the most important thing as far as my responsibilities were concerned. I came to this conclusion by what I saw leaders in the music ministry do in front of me. Everything was centered around music so if I could master that then I would be pretty set to be successful in this. I soon realized that there were some foundational things that I would have to learn quickly before I even got to the musical aspect of things. Some of these foundational things are not seen, in the open, by the public but are necessary for anyone that is truly called to lead. Every Worship leader must establish a healthy consistent prayer life with God. Prayer is necessary for every believer but it is definitely non-negotiable for the effective worship leader. We can't lead people into the presence of a Holy God if we're not consistently communicating with Him. We must be persistent in this:

"Jesus told them a story showing that it was necessary for them to pray consistently and never quit."

Luke 18:1
The Message Bible

We have to learn who God is and become familiar with His ways. How can we direct people to an intimate place with God when we haven't spent enough time with Him to really know Him? Prayer is the answer. He's very strategic and accurate but we have to constantly stay in tune with Him so that we don't detour. I'm sure you've heard the cliché, "how can you take someone to a place you've never been?" This is so true when it comes to the presence of God. We must have the ability to recognize His voice so that we are able to navigate as we LEAD. WE ARE LEADING. His presence has to be home base to us. Take a second and think, no matter where you are or where you go, home is always that place of security. It's a very familiar place; you spend time there daily. The same has to be true for God's presence.

We all have our personal preferences when it comes to styles of music but God centered worship has everything to do with what GOD wants to hear. What is moving you is null and void when God desires to hear something different. He will speak right in the middle of our worship but sometimes we miss him simply because we don't recognize His voice. Spend time with Him privately so that it's a familiar occurrence. When He begins to speak and give you instruction/direction publicly, you have the sensitivity and boldness to obey without hesitation. Our relationship with God is completely exposed when we stand before the people so it is imperative that we aren't novices when we stand before the corporate body. Solidify your prayer life. Our lack of conversing with God can cause us to miss moments of breakthrough simply due to our lack of awareness in the moment. There is a weight to this thing and we have to come back to the place where we truly value and honor the position to which we've been called. We show honor by being committed and staying on course. Pray.

My Team Must Pray Too

You can't be the only person that keeps the standard as it relates to prayer. The same has to be true for your entire team. I got saved when I was six years old and my understanding of prayer was definitely inaccurate up until I became an adult. Prayer was something that we did in the morning to thank God that we woke up or at night before we went to sleep to ask Him to keep us in tact while we were sleeping. I thought that prayer was something that you did only when you really needed something from God such as direction or blessing. I hadn't truly caught the revelation of what prayer was all about. Out of ignorance I was always in the position of asking God for something with my hands out. I very rarely spent time with him just to develop a relationship. I noticed the same was true for those that were around me as well. Some of you have found yourself in the same position when it comes to this. It doesn't mean that we don't care but it could honestly mean that we are unaware. Before you are a Worship Leader you are a child of God. He is your father and He cares about everything that matters to you because you matter so much to Him. More than telling people about Him, He desires you to tell Him what you think and how you feel about Him. When we pray these things happen. A genuine connection is inevitable at this point.

Once I started operating in a place of leadership prayer became even more important to me. There were things that I had to face that required me entering into prayer so that I could maintain my sanity through the process. As I prayed, I was able to come up with a solution for whatever circumstance I was facing. We go through and encounter things sometimes that ONLY GOD can carry us through. He is a safe place where you can voice your feelings whether you're hurt, angry, or confused. He knows it all and has the remedy! As I began to shift in this area I held my team to the same standard that I knew God was holding me to. After you have evaluated your personal prayer life you must challenge your team in the same area. They began to see an evident change not only in our ministry but they saw immediate results in their personal lives. The more they prayed, the closer they got to God. People began to look and respond differently almost immediately. Attitudes changed because there was a new awareness that came just by spending time with God. Your team's relationship with The Father is exposed just as your relationship is exposed when you lead together. *"Exposed"* doesn't have a negative connotation here but it does means that your relationship is on display. Communication is key in any relationship. Encourage your team to *TALK TO THE FATHER.*

I Understand that I Need To Pray but Am I Really An Intercessor?

We have to go back to what our actual assignment is when we are leading worship. We are to break up the fallow ground so that the Word of God can fall on good ground when it's released from the Man or Woman of God. Also, we are to help create an atmosphere that makes preaching easy for our Pastor. The truth of the matter is when we get to church for our weekly services there are spirits that meet us there. Some of these spirits are on assignment to hinder the flow of God from taking place during that gathering. Don't get it twisted; they are focused and ready to war.

For we wrestle not against flesh and blood, but against principalities, against powers, against the rulers of the darkness of this world, against spiritual wickedness in high places.

Ephesians 6:12
King James Version

There is a fresh WORD that needs to be released into our lives and if the enemy can confuse and create chaos in the atmosphere you better believe he's going to do it. When an atmosphere is filled with chaos it immediately produces distractions. We are now more focused on the distraction than we are on Worship and the Word, which is why we show up in the first place, right? We have to be aware that this isn't a fleshly battle. It's a war in the spirit and we must have knowledge and use wisdom so that we our effective in this fight. So how exactly are we supposed to fight?

For the weapons of our warfare are not physical [weapons of flesh and blood], but they are mighty before God for the overthrow and destruction of strongholds.

2 Corinthians 10:4
The Amplified Bible

To answer that question, intercession is the way that we fight. To intercede means to intervene on the behalf of. Now, with that being said every leader needs to pray for insight so that we know exactly what to confront. This is called discernment. Discernment is something that every Worship Leader should live by because again, our job is to help shift *ANY* atmosphere that we are in. There is a level of discernment that the lead worshipper must have so that we are intentional and accurate in our times of intercession. We don't always have leaders to tell us the direction that we should pray in, so we must rely on the Holy Spirit to reveal it to us. This keeps the flow in order and produces an anointing that will make worshipping and preaching easy in that atmosphere. *Remember, that's our job.*

I can remember a time where I began to sing the first song that was on our list that week in our Sunday service. There was such a heavy resistance in the atmosphere and immediately I knew we had to do something different than what we were doing at that time. Because of my ability to hear God I was able to hear Him say very clearly, "why are you trying to sing through something that you need to be interceding through?" Immediately I stopped the music and we, as a body, entered into a place of intercession. We did nothing but pray and make declarations concerning that day and immediately the yoke was broken! It took me being able to first of all hear God and then having the ability to discern so that I would know how to direct the people to intercede in that moment. Every worship leader should know that your first assignment is intercession.

Don't misunderstand me, intercession is not something that you wait to do when you get ready to lead. Intercession should happen before you get on the platform as well. Being an intercessor is a LIFE-STYLE not a momentary pleasure or fix. The cool thing about discernment and intercession is God will begin to show you things during your private time and immediately you're able to intercede on the behalf of the situation before the worship service begins. When the Holy Spirit speaks and we listen and obey, we hit the target every time. Listen to what the Apostle Paul admonishes us here:

Pray hard and long. Pray for your brothers and sisters. Keep your eyes open. Keep each other's spirits up so that no one falls behind or drops out.

Ephesians 6:18
The Message Bible

What Does Fasting Have To Do With Leading Worship?

When we participate in fasting our flesh is crucified so that our Spirit man can override our fleshly desires. It is not an easy or enjoyable process but the faithfulness of God during these times is mind blowing. The Gospel of John states that we must worship God in **Spirit** and **Truth**. This is the only way that we are truly able to worship God; it's a requirement to effectively worship Him. Worship engages your Spirit therefore we have to constantly make sure that our flesh decreases and is subject to the Spirit. *Fasting is a mandate/requirement because it allows you to hear God clearly.* The desires of our flesh can sometimes be major distractions in our lives that can prevent us from hearing the voice of God.

I can remember I was leading worship in a ministry and during a time of fasting I clearly heard God say that He was going to transition me. He immediately gave me the location and the time that He wanted me to transition. My Spirit was excited but my flesh was nervous, intimidated, and frustrated all at the same time. I had no idea what was going to happen in the natural. "I haven't received a "job offer" so where in the world will I work? My family will think I'm crazy when I tell them I'm leaving my current position strictly based upon what I heard from God". This entire time I had to remain in a place of intense prayer and fasting.

The time came for me to leave and those that were closest to me were still somewhat skeptical. It wasn't because they didn't want me to go but they were genuinely concerned with my wellbeing and only wanted the best for me. People with good pure intentions can be distractions too if you're not honed in on the voice of God. Fasting helped build my Spirit man to the point that I was able to stand on the WORD that I received from God. Through all of the questions and uncertainties I was sure of one thing, God was, is, and always will be a Man of His Word. He can't lie so if HE said it then it was up to HIM to fulfill His Word.

Once I transitioned to Orlando, Florida I went through
the first two months living off of savings. As you can imagine
I was being challenged in my faith. As difficult as it got I
never stopped fasting and praying and in two months of
being there my Pastor called me to let me know that we were
opening an additional location. He proceeded to tell me that
he wanted me to Pastor the Worship Ministry of that new
campus. At that moment it all made sense to me. I now
recognized why God gave me specifics as far as when I was
supposed to transition. Timing was extremely important in
reference to this move. If I wasn't in position I wouldn't have
been able to access what GOD had for me. He reminded me
that it is so important to not be moved by my flesh but I must
be in tune, spiritually, with what HE'S doing. Constantly
hearing what He's saying and moving according to His word.
Your flesh has to die! Fasting was killing my flesh so my Spirit

> *Fasting is a mandate/requirement because it allows you to hear God clearly.*

was free to take Dominion. That was the only thing that kept me in position during those tough times. It is, and always will be a responsibility of the Worship Leader to live a fasted lifestyle.

Afterward, when Jesus was alone in the house with his disciples, they asked him, "Why couldn't we cast out that evil spirit?" Jesus replied, "This kind can be cast out only by prayer and (fasting)."

Mark 9:28-29
New Living Translation

Principles to Remember

- *Every Worship leader must establish a healthy consistent prayer life with God.*

- *After you have evaluated your personal prayer life you must challenge your team in the same area.*

- *Every worship leader should know that your first assignment is intercession.*

- *When the Holy Spirit speaks and we listen and obey, we hit the target every time.*

- *Fasting is not optional because it allows you to hear God clearly.*

- *Your flesh has to die!*

Takeaway: My advice to you would be to make sure that every individual that serves with you understands the importance of prayer to their specific calling. It is our job as leaders to do just that, LEAD. Spend intimate time in prayer with your entire team on a regular basis. You don't have to call a special meeting, although they are sometimes necessary, to come together to seek God's face. It makes no sense for us to come together weekly to rehearse music and fail to come together weekly to seek God corporately as a team. It should be a requirement and standard for every team member to participate in these times of prayer, no exceptions. Begin every rehearsal with about 15 minutes of just interceding for the house, leadership, and the vision. This gives you an opportunity to lead your team in this capacity and it also serves as an example to them, how important prayer is to our assignment.

CHAPTER THREE

MY RELATIONSHIP WITH MY PASTOR
Submission is my Portion

Sneak Peek: This is a topic that I am excited to share and shed light on. So many Worship Leaders and Minstrels miss this next principle, which has led us to operate out of the character of God. Connecting with your Pastor and gaining his or her heart is a must if you want to please God. We are tasked to serve a vision and visionary so we must learn that submission is required. We will discuss how to operate in order when dealing with our Pastor.

Who is the ultimate Worship Leader in My Church?

I'm sure you may be wondering, *"Why is he asking who the ultimate worship leader in my church is? The person that has the task of leading worship and overseeing the area of worship is the worship leader."* This is partially correct. There is a person that is responsible for the Worship Ministry and you may be that person but the ultimate Worship Leader of every ministry is the Senior Pastor of that House. This is commonly misunderstood in ministry but has to be addressed to remain in order. This record needs to be set straight because we have a lot of worship leaders trying to be someone that they are not. Learn your role, follow instructions, and submit. God holds the Pastor accountable for every ministry within that church and every decision made concerning that church. God trusts your Pastor to shepherd every person that has made the decision to be connected to that ministry. This means that your Pastor is THE HEAD, no questions asked.

They are tasked with keeping order at all times no matter the situation because God is not the creator of confusion. If it's out of order, He's not in it. Can you believe that our Pastors have to maintain order with and minister to people who don't even want to stay in order? Rebelling just to rebel but I digress. (That's a totally different book right there). The Pastor has to remain informed at all times of the status of the Worship Ministry. The good thing about this is they don't have to micro-manage if they have leaders that have their heart and can follow through on tasks. So let me present this question to you, can your Pastor trust and depend on you to follow his instructions and not your personal preference? You are accountable to them but they are accountable to God.

> God trusts your Pastor to shepherd every person that has made the decision to be connected to that ministry.

What Happens when the Worship Team Fumbles?

So ask yourself, what happens when the Worship Leader comes in distracted or when the entire Worship team has an off day? Do we just blow it off and say we missed it today but we will get it together? Absolutely not. God holds all of us accountable for our actions but the overall responsibility falls on the shoulders of the Senior Pastor. We can't be comfortable with having "off" days because every time we step on that platform there are lives at stake. It's not just us that are affected when we allow things or emotions that have absolutely nothing to do with

God hinder us from Worshipping Him. Notice I didn't say hinder you from LEADING worship, because if you were truly worshipping you are automatically leading by example. Don't place so much energy on *"leading"* but place more energy on genuinely WORSHIPPING.

What I've learned is that some of us are failing to prepare for an encounter with God. If we didn't prepare to meet Jesus then there's no way that we have prepared to lead people to Him. In the Old Testament, you didn't just get up and go right into the presence of God without going through the required steps to enter the presence of a Holy God. There was incredible value placed on this intimate time in those days. This principle has been neglected in today's churches, which has caused us to lose reverence for HIS presence. We don't have the right to treat His presence like it's just any other place that we casually enter. We must stay in tune and aware so that we'll recognize that sanctity of those moments. It's a pure, Holy, and sacred place.

Leaders, if we decide to come to the House of God with baggage that we choose to carry, our Pastors have a very important decision to make concerning our ability to lead in that moment. The weight of that ministry still rests on their shoulders and they have a charge from GOD to care for the people and be great stewards over what they've been trusted with. Some pastors contemplate, "Do I just let them do what they feel because I don't want to hurt their feelings by confronting the situation? Or do I remain obedient to God and make sure that pure worship takes place in this gathering?" The right thing for them to do is remain obedient to God for the sake of the people and the vision. Once that conclusion is made the Pastor is now put in the position of having to correct you.

When our Pastors make the decision to take charge and correct us sometimes we choose to be offended and even upset as if they weren't justified. If we place ourselves to the side for a minute we can see the overall picture and place things into perspective. The weight of the assignment is so much bigger than your plan and your personal offenses. We must decrease so that the Spirit of God in us can rise up. That means receive the correction in love and don't leave mad at your Pastor because they rebuked and corrected you. Honestly, sometimes we just need to grow up and get over it. *Our Pastors have the duty of making sure that the sound that's being released in the house is in direct alignment with the vision and more so with what God wants to hear.*

What About My Vision for the Worship Team?

Initiative is a quality every person that leads worship should possess. It means that you will be proactive and will get things done before you are asked to do them. Individuals that take initiative are highly likely to be people that have incredible vision. They look forward and think ahead on everything that they are involved in. This is a blessing but can be detrimental if you don't use discretion. Now, depending on the individual situation, there is a level of liberty given to the Worship Leader. In most cases, we are given free reign when it comes to song selection, flow of

Worship, and the overall leading of the music ministry. On the other side you must make sure that you receive CLEAR, PRECISE direction from your Pastor so that you remain in order with the flow of where they are headed. You may be given the freedom to lead that team but it is never acceptable for you to try and make the vision of the house coincide with the vision that you have for the ministry.

We become selfish when we want things to flow the way that we desire them to flow. You must realize and accept that your vision is irrelevant at this point. *Submit your vision to the vision.* Lucifer refused to do this, which is exactly what caused him to get kicked out of Heaven. He got beside himself and thought that what He wanted (glory) was more important than God, Himself. In essence that's what you're saying when you make the decision to rebel against the visionary of the house. "God I know you speak and give my Pastor direction for my church but this is what I WANT to do with the Worship Ministry. As you read that it sounded pretty ridiculous didn't it? Allow this to cause you to really evaluate if you are helping fulfill the vision or if you're coming in and causing DIVISION. When this spirit rises, it's an automatic sign that there is an issue with submission.

Your Yes Makes Life Easier for Your Pastor

Worship Leaders can be an incredible asset to the life of a Pastor or they can be one of the biggest thorns in the life of a Pastor. The enemy loves to create division and confusion in this relationship because anything that remains divided can't stand together. The Pastor and Worship Leader work so closely together that it is necessary for there to be a certain level of chemistry between the two. Lucifer hates the Worshipper because we have the opportunity to do what he once did. It makes him angry when he thinks about the fact that we have direct access to God at any given time! Knowing this, it is not surprising that rebellion and lack of submission is prevalent in the worship ministry. Those two terms are synonymous with Lucifer's name. He basically lost his mind and refused to submit to God. When we refuse to submit to the Head of the house we are not only dishonoring them but we are dishonoring God. The bible tells us to view no man after the flesh so we must submit ourselves to the GOD that's inside of our Pastors. It's bigger than an individual.

The mistake that we as leaders make, as it pertains to submission, is we feel like we have to agree and/or understand the instruction that's being given. This statement is 100% inaccurate. You know what's crazy? *When you choose to honor and obey your leader, even when they're missing God, God will in return honor your obedience.* The only exception to that principle is if you are being instructed to do something that is contrary to The Word of God. The flip side of that is if your leader misses God and you rebel, you are now held accountable for not obeying a principle of God. Every leader needs to ask themselves, *"Do I resemble Lucifer?"* If there is any hesitation or if you answer is yes then your next step is to repent and course correct that area.

Be responsive to your pastoral leaders. Listen to their counsel. They are alert to the condition of your lives and

work under the strict supervision of God. Contribute to the joy of their leadership, not its drudgery. Why would you want to make things harder for them?

Hebrews 13:17
The Message Bible

Earlier I stated that God is a God of order so that means that He gives directions to your Pastor concerning the church, not you. Your Pastor is the mouthpiece of God for the House and for your life and that position is to be honored. Some of us are having trouble because

> *When you choose to honor and obey your leader, even when they're missing God, God will in return honor your obedience.*

we are prostituting our gifts with no true connection with the vision or visionary of the House. If you are in a ministry and that Pastor is not the mouthpiece of God for your life then you are in the wrong place. Don't be a hireling and continue to say things like *"well I work at this church but this is the church that I belong to."* This is **OUT OF ORDER** and has to be stopped in the House of God. We've adopted this "gig" mentality strictly for money and have lost sight of why we do what we do. Go somewhere and connect because of the WORD that's going forth in that house not because of a certain amount of money that they're willing to give you. Submit your gift to that house.

If you aren't submitted to GOD in reference to where you're supposed to be then you won't be able to submit to the GOD that is inside of any Pastor. Something is unlocked when we submit to Spiritual Authority. God intervenes and moves on our behalf. He will favor you and bless you in ways that you could never imagine simply because you have given him a "Yes." Your willingness to be obedient will always take you through doors that your gift will never be able to get you in. What good is talent with no influence? Take a second to think about that. If you're uncomfortable or vexed reading this section as we are discussing submission don't tune the HOLY SPIRIT out. This could be a great opportunity for you to submit to God first and make this thing right. Allow God to release you from that, even in this very moment. If you need to go back and reread it until you catch the revelation don't ignore the Holy Ghost. This is the last day that you will operate in rebellion and be ok with it. No more. There's far too much work to be done in the Kingdom! BE RESTORED!

I've done That and Seen No Change... What Now?

Honestly, there are some cases where you have people that serve in leadership positions in the music ministry and it seems that they can never stay on the same page as their Pastor. If you should ever find yourself in this situation you must sit and evaluate the big picture. The first thing you've got to do is go back to the Word that God spoke to you that caused you to be in that position from the start. Secondly, you need to make sure that you have humbled yourself and are not operating from a prideful place. Have you taken initiative and tried to talk to your Pastor? Remember, it is your job to pursue your Pastor not the other way around. If you have pursued him, how many times have you tried? Did you get disappointed or frustrated when you tried twice and didn't get the response that you wanted? If your answer is multiple times and you've changed your approach each time and you still haven't seen a change, then it's time to go back in your prayer closet for guidance as it pertains to your next move.

If you've prayed fervently and with diligence and God hasn't given you instructions to move then you stay right where you are and continue to submit and obey. It's very dangerous to move on your own will. He will send your deliverance in the form of God rectifying that situation or removing you from the situation. There can be a valuable lesson that He is requiring you to learn before he releases you into your next. That's why it is important to let GOD do it and keep your hands out of it. If He gives you a Word then HE has to fulfill that Word, but if you go on your own intellect and *"experience"* then you could end up in trouble. We can be guilty of doing our own thing without consulting God sometimes and then beg, plead, and even have the nerve to get frustrated with Him when we continuously meet opposition. If you weren't SENT and you just decided to go then you've got to take responsibility for that action that you took upon yourself to make. *Never expect God to tell you to stop doing something that HE NEVER told you to do in the first place.*

Then Peter called to him, "Lord, if it's really you, tell me to come to you, walking on the water." "Yes, come," Jesus said.

St. Matthew 14:28-29
New Living Translation

Principles to Remember

- The weight of the assignment is so much bigger than your plan and your personal offenses.

- Our Pastors have the duty of making sure that the sound that's being released in the house is in direct alignment with the vision and more so with what God wants to hear.

- You may be given the freedom to lead that team but it is never acceptable for you to try and make the vision of the house coincide with the vision that you have for the ministry.

- Submit your vision to the vision.

- Worship Leaders can be an incredible asset to the life of a Pastor or they can be one of the biggest thorns in the life of a Pastor.

- When you choose to honor and obey your leader, even when they're missing God, God will in return honor your obedience.

- If you aren't submitted to GOD in reference to where you're supposed to be then you won't be able to submit to the GOD that is inside of any Pastor.

- Never expect God to tell you to stop doing something that HE NEVER told you to do in the first place.

Takeaway: I would encourage you to make sure that there is an open line of communication between you and your Pastor.

Communication needs to be a consistent thing just to ensure that you stay on the same page. It's always better to over communicate rather than not communicating enough. It is your job to go to them not the other way around. Don't be afraid to ask questions and don't be too bull-headed to receive correction. Correction doesn't mean that there is a personal issue; it just means things need to change. As I said earlier, keep the communication with you and God open as well. Make sure that you are right where He wants you to be. You can't judge the situation based on the way that you feel but you can find the answer by seeking HIS face. When you have a Word you have a firm foundation to stand on when things don't appear to be favorable. If you missed God don't allow pride to keep you in a position because you refuse to admit that you were wrong. The positive way to look at "missing God" is that you have enough God in you to be able to recognize that you may have missed Him.

CHAPTER FOUR

I WAS NOT CREATED TO BE AN ISLAND
Relationships and Mentorship

Sneak Peek: I will have to say that this is my favorite section out of this book. For me, the road to finding this was a long road but once I caught this principle my life immediately changed forever. Relationships are so important in the Kingdom. We are going to talk about how to identify those key, God ordained relationships that catapult you into your destiny.

Do I Really Need Relationships?

In some instances singers, musicians, and yes-even Worship Leaders can be the most territorial people you meet. We are gifted individuals but it seems to be somewhat common to meet extremely gifted people that are lacking in people skills. We are professionals at conversing about what we've accomplished and what we're currently doing but it's rare for us to want genuine relationships. As long as we are talking about musically related things we are ok but as soon as a serious conversation about life comes we shut down.

Psalmist and Minstrels have been allowed to do this for so long because many people value the gift more than the person that contains the gift. It's an attitude of "I'll leave you alone as long as you come in and use your gift to do what I need". Many things that are detrimental to a person's ministry and life are overlooked for the sake of what they have to offer. This is the poor mentality that has caused many to ultimately fail. You need someone in your life that will vow to always speak the truth in love.

When the truth is spoken in love it doesn't always feel good to us but there's no doubt that it is good for us. Having people that are selfless enough to help you by being truthful builds a level of trust between you and those individuals. We, as Levites, also tend to sometimes have a difficult time asking for help or assistance. We allow our pride to make us feel like we should know everything concerning our area of ministry. I've even found that this is not only true in ministry but sometimes life in general. Asking someone for help does not mean that you are inadequate in any way. God can decide to use some one that you are in relationship with to give you an answer that you've been seeking him for. Failure to cultivate and utilize these relationships can again stifle progress.

> **As iron sharpens iron, so a friend sharpens a friend.**
> **Proverbs 27:17**
> **New Living Translation**

I think that it's important for us to identify what things may keep us from cultivating relationships. It could be because of insecurities that we don't want people to be aware of or it could be because we have tried in the past and for whatever reason, weren't successful. Both of these are very valid concerns but they shouldn't be used as an excuse from moving on and trying again. I do think that the most common reason that we procrastinate on developing relationships is *pride*. The Bible says that *"pride comes before the fall"*. I like to think of it this way, **pride is me being full of who I am but confidence is me recognizing who God is in me**. But why is pride so prevalent in the Music Ministry? We have to visit the character of Lucifer to answer this question.

Pride comes in a few different forms and both of these forms are enemies of your relationships. You can take on the attitude of I don't really have the desire to have anyone tell me what I should know or you can be the person that's so secretive because you don't want anyone knowing what you know. I've found that some people are too nervous to teach

> Pride is me being full of who I am but confidence is me recognizing who God is in me.

another individual what they know because there is a fear of that individual getting a better opportunity than they have. We are all supposed to have the same focus and goals in ministry but now instead of working together we are being secretive and ultimately competing. So we have one group that's too prideful to receive the help that they need and another group that is too prideful to release the help that needs to flow from them. It has now become all about you and God is nowhere to be found. Say this, "it's really not all about me." Always remember that two is better than one! It is not the Will of God for any of us to live on an island. HE didn't create you to be by yourself all the time. This idea of "I'm good and don't really need anyone to help" has placed our area of ministry in the zone where there is no accountability.

Accountability is needed but NEVER "feels" good when you have to answer to someone for your actions or lack thereof. We need people that can critique and correct us so that we can walk and operate on level that God has purposed for us to be on. Who do you have in your life that can tell you no? After reading this, if a few names didn't come to mind it could be an indicator that you need to make yourself accountable to someone. It's also an indicator that a **mentor** is needed in your life immediately. *A mentor can help guide you and keep you on the straight and narrow if you choose to listen.* They are people that are committed to telling you the truth without fear of what you may think about their observation. Mentorship is a personal developmental relationship in which a more experienced or more knowledgeable person helps to guide a less experienced or less knowledgeable person. No matter who you are or what you do, it is imperative for you to have at least one mentor in your life.

> *Accountability is needed but NEVER "feels" good when you have to answer to someone for your actions or lack thereof.*

The Journey to Realizing I needed a Mentor

I began leading in music ministry at the age of 11. I had the responsibility of choosing music as well as teaching all parts for all four choirs in the church. As you can imagine it was an interesting position to be in because 85% of the people were old enough to be my parents. I never had anyone blatantly disrespect me because my age but I did find myself in situations that weren't the most comfortable. I was still a kid but I had taken on the responsibility of an adult. Adults respected me for who I was and what I was anointed to do but at the end of the day I was still a kid to them. All of the kids my age looked at me as if I was much older than them, so I struggled to find out where I fit in. My battle was this, I felt like I was too mature to do silly things that kids my age did but not old enough to be included with the adults. I knew what I was there to do, but I still struggled to find my place. Ever felt this way? When we aren't in the right relationships, no matter what crowd you are a part of, you have this void that you have to fill.

This was the hardest part about the position that I was in. I needed someone that could understand where I was, recognize the call that was on my life, and help direct me through this process. God had started speaking to me very clearly in my youth but I needed someone to help me sort through what I was sensing and hearing.

Then God called out, "Samuel, Samuel!" Samuel answered, "Yes? I'm here." Then he ran to Eli saying, "I heard you call. Here I am." Eli said, "I didn't call you. Go back to bed." And so he did. God called again, "Samuel, Samuel!" Samuel got up and went to Eli, "I heard you call. Here I am." Again Eli said, "Son, I didn't call you. Go back to bed." (This all happened before Samuel knew God for himself. It was before the revelation of God had been given to him personally.) God called again, "Samuel!"—the third time! Yet again Samuel got up and went to Eli, "Yes? I heard you call me. Here I am." That's when it dawned on Eli that God was calling the boy. So Eli directed Samuel, "Go back and lie down. If the voice calls again, say, 'Speak, God. I'm your servant, ready to listen.'" Samuel returned to his bed.

1 Samuel 3:4-9
The Message Bible

I don't think that I was familiar with the term mentor at this point of my life but that's exactly what I longed for. I wanted a person to speak into my life and care more about me than what I was gifted to do. It's a difficult thing as a child or adult to operate in your call consistently hurting or just having questions that are never answered. I searched for this in a couple of people and without fail I was let down every time. I don't feel that this was on purpose or malicious but I think a lot of times people only do what they know. I learned a very valuable rule. *You can't force a connection with a mentor but it has to be a God ordained.*

There are definitely times where we all have questions that may be simple but you need to ask someone that has experience in what you're doing. Understand now that it doesn't make you weak nor does it put your "validity" in question. It actually means that you are smart enough to ask someone that has the knowledge and wisdom that you need. That's much easier than having to go through the process to learn. *Humbling yourself and asking questions is definitely the way to go.*

There are so many scripture references that lets us know that it's okay to have someone help us.

It's better to have a partner than go it alone. Share the work, share the wealth. And if one falls down, the other helps, But if there's no one to help, tough!

Ecclesiastes 4:9-10
The Message Bible

Identify, Pursue, and Establish

I think that in life we all have several different people that we look up to. Whether you're involved in sports, music, or any other extracurricular activity you have someone that you admire. This person is often found in the public eye, you may not know them personally but you watch very closely to learn different things. These people are easily visible so they become examples by default. It's great to have different influences because it helps you stay fresh and keeps you from becoming mundane. The fault in this is a lot of people have mistaken this for mentorship. It's not a bad thing to do but we must know that this is not mentorship. *In order for a person to mentor you, you must have a relationship with them.* They have to help lead you in the right direction so they have to KNOW YOU. You have to converse with them so that they can be aware of where you are in life and what's happening with you. I've always said that mentors have the ability to cut you. They are present during your pruning stages so they have to recognize and be familiar with who you really are.

Now I'm sure we all have different stories that we can tell in relation to how we met our mentors. I think that my story may be a little different from some though. I knew of my mentor for about 5 years before I officially met him. I heard of the things that God was doing through their ministry for years before I ever attended the church. I remember in 2006 I attended a Camp Meeting at the church where he was serving and I was really focused on the way that He led and navigated through the service. I had no idea that Three years later God would speak to both of us concerning our assignment to each other. In the summer of 2008 I left my home church and I made the decision to disobey God and not connect to the ministry that He instructed me to connect to. It wasn't until the beginning of 2009 where I knew I had to stop running and submit to GOD. I was sitting in a service listening to the Pastor preach and heard God say "Go to Pastor Brinson and tell him you're coming to rehearsal tomorrow". There's significance behind that word that God spoke to me. I had searched for a mentor and a Spiritual father for so long that I had gotten accustomed to the thought of rejection. It had crippled me to the point to where I no longer knew how to go to someone and say "listen this is what I need. My confidence had been ruined over the years.

Although, I did want to connect with the music ministry, that wasn't my sole purpose for being there. I KNEW in that moment when God spoke to me that there was something on Pastor Brinson's life that had to be released to me. As soon as church was over I knew I couldn't procrastinate. I prayed a quick prayer and asked God to go before me so that he would be prepared when I approached him. I don't think that I could have handled another rejection. Church hurt is a different type of pain that a person never becomes immune to. Have you ever been hurt in church? If so, you can be healed. So, I walked up to him and spoke and said, "Hey sir, I will be in rehearsal tomorrow night." He responded and said, "Wow ok... we need to talk?" and at that moment I knew that He was my mentor and Spiritual Father.

You are probably wondering how I was able to conclude

that after that simple dialogue. You know, there's something really unique about fathers and mothers when it comes to their children. They know what they're children are really saying and asking for, even when they don't come right out and say it. I didn't go and ask him to mentor me I simply said that I was coming to rehearsal but God revealed to him what I truly needed. In that moment God not only answered my prayer that I had been praying for years but He also restored my confidence in Him. I took a step of faith and He honored it. God will always honor your obedience.

This was only the beginning to me learning how to be a mentee. There were many sacrifices that I had to make in order to receive everything that God wanted me to receive from this God ordained relationship. I began to travel with him and literally pick his brain about different things concerning ministry and life. *Mentorship has little to do with what you do but it has all to do with who you are.* I'm sure there were times where he was probably thinking, "I wish this boy would leave me alone for a little while". I'd prayed for so long that I had more zeal and enthusiasm about my assignment and life more than I ever had. I wasn't going to miss any opportunity to learn and grow. There is power in being connected to the right people. What makes them right people? They are people that God as specifically ordained to be in your life. He orchestrates things in a way that your paths cross. God is amazing.

I want you to take everything that I've shared in this chapter and apply it. If you have yet to find your mentor don't give up. Petition God and allow Him to lead you right into the path that you need to walk in. He knows exactly what and whom you need in your life. If you do have a mentor or if you know who they are and have yet to establish a relationship with them, procrastinate no longer. You can be withholding your destiny simply because you you're not taking advantage of what is right in front of you. You can't do this alone, no matter how hard you try. None of us are that "good".

Receive your double portion!

And when they had gone over, Elijah said to Elisha, Ask what I shall do for you before I am taken from you. And Elisha said, I pray you, let a double portion of your spirit be upon me.

2 Kings 2:9
The Amplified Bible

Principles to Remember

- Accountability is needed but NEVER "feels" good when you have to answer to someone for your actions or lack thereof.
- No matter who you are or what you do, it is imperative for you to have at least one mentor in your life.
- You can't force a connection with a mentor but it has to be a God ordained.
- Humbling yourself and asking questions is definitely the way to go.
- In order for a person to mentor you, you must have a relationship with them.
- Mentorship has little to do with what you do but it has all to do with who you are.

Takeaway: Don't avoid relationships that can help prune and fine-tune you. These relationships won't always feel the best but in order to get to the place of maturity you need them. Mentors are a blessing from the Father. Mentors will sometime seem like your tormentors but God has given them insight on how to help equip you for your next level. Identify who these individuals are and establish a consistent connection.

CHAPTER FIVE

IDENTIFYING MY STRONG POINTS
As A Worship Leader

Sneak Peek: It's time for us to identify who we are, individually, as worship leaders. We are going to discuss how we can capitalize on areas that we excel in. We will also find out what we should do when there is a need in an area that we aren't fully equipped to meet. Once you identify your personalized niche, it is then when you will be able to lead from a place of security. Walking in the boldness of who God has called YOU to be is the only EFFECTIVE way to do this.

I've Got To Be Me

We hear this all of the time, but when you actually sit and think about it, there is really no place like the Presence of God. No other place even compares or comes close to comparing to His presence. One of the things that I truly love about God is I am able to come to Him just as I am. He made me and knows every intricate detail about me so there's absolutely no point of putting up a facade. He's not interested in me acting as if I'm perfect because He's fully aware that I'm not. Disguises are not needed nor are they wanted when we come to worship Him in *Spirit and Truth*. His presence rectifies everything. There's no way that you can have a true encounter with God and remain the same. In other words, anything that isn't "right" is made right in His presence. He just wants you, the real you!

It's who you are and the way you live that count before God. Your worship must engage your spirit in the pursuit of truth. That's the kind of people the Father is out looking for: those who are simply and honestly themselves before him in their worship. God is sheer being itself—Spirit. Those who worship him must do it out of their very being, their spirits, their true selves, in adoration.

John 4:23-24
The Message Bible

In chapter 3 we talked a little about mentorship. We defined mentorship and also identified that it was different from admiration. Being influenced and gleaning from someone is a positive thing and can be very beneficial to us. As we work to grow as leaders, having a guide to look to allows us to have a solid starting point. This is helpful during those times when things get difficult and challenging. *We must be very careful that we don't step into the place of mimicking the people that we admire. There is a way to adopt similarities but still maintain your individuality.* There is no need for imitation in the Kingdom because we have been strategically equipped and designed. God hasn't called any two people to be exactly the same because that would ultimately mean that someone is not needed.

There is a unique assignment, calling, and anointing that God has released to every one of us. When we come before people to minister, we need The Father to place His stamp of approval on us. This "stamp" is His anointing, which is what draws people near to Him. We are simply vessels that are submitted to Him so that He's able to move and flow freely. *Before God is able to anoint you, He first has to be able to recognize you.* He doesn't recognize you if you're altering your actions and manipulating your way of doing things to resemble someone else's style. *Authenticity is a prerequisite that is needed in order to receive the oil.* It's about who you really are, not who you pretend to be. *God's anointing can only rest on the REAL you.* You have to come to the place where you can be comfortable in who YOU are in Him.

If you look at the universal Worship/ Music ministry, you'll find that we have so many people that are battling identity crises. You will never reach the place that God has ordained for you to reach if you operate as someone that you're not. Our true identity is found in who God is in our lives. Know the will of God for YOUR life and be secure in who He is. He is that place of refuge and security. I love to describe God as a "safe place". There are no inadequacies or discrepancies with God because He is a SURE God!

Make this vow to Him today and everyday thereafter:

"God, from this day forward I will acknowledge, appreciate, and place value on who you have called ME to be."

Strengths and Weaknesses

I think it's amazing how God created each of us in our own unique way. I truly believe that He designed us in a way in which we would soon realize that no matter what we embarked upon, we need the assistance of the people around us. Even as we settle into who we are He still reveals how those around us can assist us. We've all begun a process, and whether you've gone a quarter of the way or even halfway, you've met a roadblock that would force you to ask for help or guidance. In these processes we learn very vital things about ourselves. It proves what we do and do not know. An assessment of us is taken whether we ask for it or not. A major thing that we detect during this assessment is our strengths and weaknesses.

We must be very careful that we don't step into the place of mimicking the people that we admire. There is a way to adopt similarities but still maintain your individuality.

Before, we talked about realizing that we need help from those that we're connected to, and the weaknesses in our lives serve as a great reminder of that principle. It's pretty difficult to watch an individual struggle to operate in an area that they are weak in. It's extremely easy to discern and can even be a hindrance depending on the circumstance and setting. It's almost as if you get the feeling that they are forcing something that seems to be extremely difficult or even impossible at that time. Some gifts and talents God has given us just come natural, and we don't have to put forth extreme effort to execute them, Then we have those other things that we are gifted in but require a little more attention and effort to bring to the place of excellence. Fine-tuning and cultivating the gift brings that gift to a higher level of excellence. *It's beneficial to the Worship Leader to capitalize on strengths as you're enhancing those weaker areas.*

Once strengths are identified it is of the utmost importance that you begin to bring those things to the forefront, immediately. As you exercise and put them to work you are creating a system that ultimately makes those strengths stronger. There is always room to enhance and improve. Let me give you a few examples. If you know as a Worship Leader your strengths are Song leading and prophetic flow then capitalize on those two areas. Lead and flow at the level that God has given you the capacity to flow in. I love to think of it this way; those things that come easy to us are natural, right? But now think about this, when God takes our weaknesses combined with our strengths and His anointing, we are now ministering at a Supernatural level. That level is totally beyond our comprehension and makes us a vessel that God can be 100% effective through. It's almost as if we say to Him, "Ok God, I'm going to give you something to work with, I'll do my part." Once He has your cooperation He can do ANYTHING through you. Don't neglect those weaker areas but you definitely want to make sure that you execute these strong areas with persistency and boldness.

So I'm sure your next question is, *what do I do in the areas that I'm not so strong in? What happens as I'm working to get stronger?* I'm excited that you asked. As I previously stated, you definitely want to make sure that you solidify those strengths in the beginning stages. But after you are established, you must make sure that you give as much attention, time, and effort to your weaknesses as you do your strengths. To be honest, there may need to be a little more effort put towards those weaker areas to bring them up to par. This is really the only way that we will succeed in making them stronger. The only issue with this is that while you're growing in that area there can be a high demand for whatever that thing is. So, let's say teaching parts and administration are areas that you are weak in, what do you do? As a leader you have the responsibility to deliver, so the responsibility rests on you. You don't have the luxury to bring things to a halt until you are ready to proceed. Things must flow, move, and progress at a steady pace. So what do you do in the mean time? The best thing that you can do is pull on the people connected to you that are exceptionally strong in the areas that you're weak.

In the previous chapter, I expressed the importance of relationships and now you will better understand my purpose for doing so. A very popular quote that we hear now is "teamwork makes the dream work."2 I love this saying because it constantly reminds me of the people that God has connected me with.

You can easily enough see how this kind of thing works by looking no further than your own body. Your body has many parts—limbs, organs, cells—but no matter how many parts you can name, you're still one body. It's exactly the same with Christ.

1 Corinthians 12:12
The Message Bible

If you expect everything to come from one place (you) you will miss the whole concept of what vision really is. Real vision is and will forever be so much greater than one individual. It has everything to do with every person bringing what they have to the table, to help bring the vision to past. Vision is so powerful that it outlives an individual and even continues to progress even after the visionary is gone.

As a leader, you have to be able to assess your team/ circle and recognize the strengths of those around you. This is not the time to be intimidated, but it's the perfect chance for you to realize that God placed them there for this very reason. The entire body is needed to function at its best potential. No organ or limb is any less important than any other, but if you don't have one of these organs or limbs the entire body may suffer. Those of us that serve are a body and it's important that we all operate in whatever we have been anointed and gifted to do. He created you so HE knows what you are and are not capable of. Instead of leaving you high and dry he brings someone alongside of you that can fulfill those needs. He'll show you your ram in the bush so that you don't have struggle or be sacrificed.

Principles to Remember

- We must be very careful that we don't step into the place of mimicking the people that we admire. There is a way to adopt similarities but still maintain your individuality.

- Before God is able to anoint you, He first has to be able to recognize you.

- Authenticity is a prerequisite that is needed in order to receive the oil.

- God's anointing can only rest on the REAL you.

- It's beneficial to the Worship Leader to capitalize on strengths as you're enhancing those weaker areas.

Takeaway: I think more than anything, I want you to finish this chapter knowing that because GOD has anointed you, you are adequate. There is no need to feel like you need to be someone else or be someone that you're not. When God does something He does it well, and that is the way that you have to perceive yourself. Be confident in His ability! Every area that you are strong in, maximize your potential in those areas! Any area that you are weak in, pull on the people around you as you work to make them better!

CHAPTER SIX

KEEPING IT REAL
There's a Practical Side to What We Do

Sneak Peek: Now it's time for us to dive into some practical things. After we have the foundational things set in order, we must dissect the practical side of leading worship and leading as a whole. From team selection, to rehearsals, to team building we will discuss techniques and principles that work to build a great team and produce chemistry and effectiveness.

Let's Get Practical

After you've established a firm foundation with prayer, submission to the vision and visionary, and a healthy relationship with mentors and Spiritual influences, there's more that has to be done to put you in a place of effectiveness. There are some very practical things that can be done to produce trust with your team and order in your ministry. It is necessary for the Worship Leader/ Pastor to have systems in place to maintain consistency. From music to administration, every worship leader is responsible for the flow of things. I wanted to take a moment and discuss those tools and practical things that I've found helpful over the years. Implementing these things have not brought perfection, but they have brought results and consistency. Our goal is to be effective, so let's talk about it.

Choosing Your Team

Church is one of the few places that we allow people to do what they want without course correcting them. *As a leader, you have the responsibility to tell people the truth even if its contrary to what they may feel or think.* God has given us insight, and He trusts us to release that insight to those that we are responsible for leading. Sometimes people have a false perception of what they're gifted in because someone previously lied to them. Over the years, I have definitely found this to be true for our area of ministry. When selecting your team you have many areas that need to be evaluated so you have an accurate view of whom you are dealing with. So, how do you go about selecting a team to serve and lead with you? First and foremost, you must know whether they have the gift of music. The Bible states that David was anointed and skilled so that gift needs to be evident in us.

Saul told his servants, "Go ahead. Find me someone who can play well and bring him to me." One of the young men spoke up, "I know someone. I've seen him myself: the son of Jesse of Bethlehem, an excellent musician. He's also courageous, of age, well-spoken, and good-looking. And God is with him." So Saul sent messengers to Jesse requesting, "Send your son David to me, the one who tends the sheep."

1 Samuel 16:17-19
The Message Bible

There is absolutely nothing wrong with taking EVERY member through an audition process. A lot of people in ministry dislike this and sometimes shy away from it, but it will save you some trouble in the long run. We worry sometimes about offending someone, or hurting their feelings but you are hurting them if you allow them to operate in an area that they are equipped in. The awesome thing is if they are not a right fit for the Worship Ministry there are many different opportunities for them to serve in other ministries. *If you audition an individual that does not possess the gift of music, you have an awesome opportunity to help redirect them.* Find their strengths and interests and PASTOR/LEAD them into the direction where they can be effective. Remember, you aren't just a leader when you stand with a microphone or instrument in your hand. If you commit to telling them the truth they will eventually thank you for it.

> *As a leader, you have the responsibility to tell people the truth even if it's contrary to what they may feel or think.*

It is refreshing when you complete an audition with someone that has an incredible gift. We are music lovers so we are drawn to quality and skill. There is still more that needs to be evaluated and discussed after you discover the gift. Who are they? Where did they come from?

Why do they want to be connected to the Worship Ministry? *You must have an initial face-to-face meeting with every potential member on your team.* During this time, you are able to ask all of these questions and get to know the person behind the gift. Some gifts and personalities/ attitudes resemble each other, but sometimes this is the complete opposite. Ever met a person with a gift that is ten times better than their attitude? I have and it's normally pretty evident from the beginning of a conversation. You must tune in.

It's always good to allow them to talk as you listen, evaluate, and discern. You'll find that most of the time this person has gone through something that has caused them to react in this negative manner. There's a great possibility they've been hurt, offended, or torn down. This means that they need to go through a healing and restoration process, and you must ALWAYS be OPEN to assisting them through this. If you find that they are willing to go through that process, you have the honor of being a catalyst to their deliverance. This could be a short or long process depending on the individual, but continue to have an open mind and willing heart to stick it out as long as they WANT deliverance. I will be honest this takes a great deal of patience. *Always remember, someone has been and will have to be patient with you.*

Always be humble and gentle. Be patient with each other, making allowance for each other's faults because of your love.

Ephesians 4:2
New Living Translation

So, what happens when you do everything that you can to help but you are rejected? There's something about help and deliverance that we all have to understand. The person that needs help has to genuinely WANT it. They've got to want it for themselves even more than you want it for them. Don't allow discouragement to creep in when you meet resistance. There are times where God uses us to simply plant the seed. In due time, HE will move on their heart and use someone else to help water the seed. Continue to pray for that individual because GOD can totally transform them. The next time you see them you could see a completely healed and whole person standing in front of you. Just make sure that you are obedient in fulfilling your role in the situation.

Rehearsals

Have you ever sat in a rehearsal that was so unorganized you wondered how the team would be able to pull things together before service? It seems as if no one has a clue of what's going on. This has definitely happened to me several times. It made me evaluate the overall picture and realize that the things that happen beforehand are vital to the delivery on service days. We don't just show up and find things in place the way that they should be. There's some groundwork that has to be done. *Rehearsals, meetings, and overall preparation for the worship experience determine the ease of your flow.* If there is confusion and disorganization during your rehearsals the same will be true for your services. What we see during service is a representation of what happened in rehearsal and before you entered the sanctuary.

So, let's back up and talk a little more in depth about rehearsals. The first thing that you need to do is make sure that your entire team (singers, musicians, sound, etc.) knows when and where your rehearsals are held. This may sound like a no-brainer, but you would be surprised that there are people a part of Worship teams that have to guess when rehearsal will be. You can imagine that this produces frustration before members even get to rehearsal, which brings immediate opposition. There is a spirit of confusion simply because there was a lack of communication. *Lack of communication leads to frustration, which leads to offense.* It's always best to over communicate. It may be annoying to some, but you will never have to deal with anyone saying that they were unaware of something. If you make sure everyone is aware of your plans you are on the right track.

You also want to make sure that everyone has the material that you cover in those rehearsals. There is a smooth flow when everyone has a road map of where they are going in that session, and it enables everyone to have the opportunity to come prepared. This can literally knock off thirty minutes to an hour of rehearsal time. Most worship team members are volunteers so you want to be mindful of that when it comes to their time. I have a rule that I abide by with all of my team members. I require them to know lyrics and the melody for all songs that are covered. This serves as a great assistance to me when it's time to teach harmonies because everyone has an understanding of where we're going.

Work hard so you can present yourself to God and receive his approval. Be a good worker, one who does not need to be ashamed and who correctly explains the word of truth.

2 Timothy 2:15
New Living Translation

Before You Stand

NEVER task your team to attempt to execute a song that YOU KNOW they are not ready for at that time. You build confidence in them when they are able to learn and conquer a song, but you do the complete opposite when they feel that they have failed. You must keep this in mind because depending on the maturity level of your team this could "make or break" the way that they view their gifts. Your team loves the sense of accomplishment that they feel when they've done a good job. You are their leader, so they value your opinion, sometimes more than you may realize!

Team Building

We have already talked about the value that we should place on relationships in our lives. This remains true when you talk about the Worship ministry/ team (singers, musicians, dancers, etc.). *Team building is an area that isn't addressed often, but it is extremely necessary for any team.* Friction and misunderstandings sometimes come simply because we don't genuinely know people. Also, knowing your

83

team outside of music and ministry will increase your level of effectiveness. This will produce chemistry and flow that will allow you to press through any atmosphere. I'm sure we all have spent time with people and found ourselves in a situation where we say, "I knew you were going to do that." This is possible because you have spent enough time with that person to learn their ways. When they did what they did, it wasn't foreign to you because you've caught on to the way they operate.

Most worship teams, choirs, etc. meet at least once a week for rehearsals. People have a chance to see each other and have small talk but this isn't the time to really get to know a person. Every team should spend time together outside of the four walls of their church. Rehearsals and meetings are great, but there is a need for gatherings outside of that. Game nights are something that I've done for years. You can count on at least one person showing a different side of them that you may not see on a weekly basis. This automatically makes people feel closer to that person, and it makes that person feel more comfortable with the entire team. Board games bring out the competitive silly side of people. *Try it!* There is a chance that maybe your team won't want to play board games. There are other options such as bowling or a team outing (mall, amusement park, fair, carnival). If none of these work there is definitely one thing that I am positive will work with EVERY TEAM. No matter who you are and what you enjoy doing there is something that we all have in common. We all love to eat! Church people will make up a reason to have refreshments or meal (lol). It may sound comical, but you honestly learn things about people that you may have never known when you sit a table to eat with them. Breaking bread is the quickest way to find out what a person thinks and how they really feel. You'll find that these become some of the best ministry opportunities. In spite of where the conversation began it always seems to turn right back to GOD. These times are so important for us individually, but it's also important to our flow on the platform. The Bible tells us to "know them that labor among you." Making the honest effort to talk to and care about your brother and sister that you serve with will produce something that no other action can produce. It creates the Spirit of unity within your team. We have to walk in unity in order for the true manifested Presence of God to rest over us.

Behold, how good and how pleasant it is for brethren to dwell together in unity!

Psalm 133:1
The Amplified Bible

Principles to Remember

- As a leader, you have the responsibility to tell people the truth even if its contrary to what they may feel or think.

- There is absolutely nothing wrong with taking EVERY member through an audition process.

- If you audition an individual that does not possess the gift of music, you have an awesome opportunity to help redirect them.

- You must have an initial face-to-face meeting with every potential member on your team.

- Always remember, someone has been and will have to be patient with you.

- Rehearsals, meetings, and overall preparation for the worship experience determine the ease of your flow.

- Lack of communication leads to frustration, which leads to offense.

- NEVER task your team to attempt to execute a song that YOU KNOW they are not ready for at that time.

- Team building is an area that isn't addressed often, but it is extremely necessary for any team.

Takeaway: There are many ways to handle things but you can always refer back to this section if you have a practical issue. These principles will make the Worship Ministry in your house effective if implemented.

CHAPTER SEVEN
THE PRINCIPLE THAT CAN'T BE TAUGHT

I have given you what I believe to be the foundation of Leading and serving in the Worship and Arts ministry. These principles can assist you in enhancing your gift and becoming comfortable in your calling. I want to encourage you to make sure that you stay before God. He gives accurate instruction that is catered to your specific situation. There are things that I can't teach you and truthfully no one will be able to teach you. One of the greatest influences in my life told me something years ago. She said, "Some things are caught not taught." That principle stuck with me and has served as a constant reminder that I need to stay in tune with what God is saying and doing. Your relationship with God is what will keep you when things around you seem to be unstable. HE really is the SOLID ROCK! Never forget that the Word of God and your prayer life are the two things that will keep you on course. *Stay the course!*

ACKNOWLEDGMENTS

This is probably one of the most difficult things for me to do because there are so many individuals that have been instrumental in helping to mold me into the man that I am today.

First, I have to thank *my parents* for being two of my biggest supporters for the past twenty-eight years. You have unselfishly given your time, advice, resources, and love since I can remember. You've instilled principles in me that I will never forget! To *my sister and brother-in-law*, thank you for ALWAYS being there to encourage me and help me see the greatness in me even when I was unable to recognize it. I LOVE YOU ALL!

To my *Pastor, David Brinson, and First Lady, April Brinson*, (mentors) you are not only my Pastors but also my Spiritual father and mother. I pray that every Spiritual son and daughter have the opportunity to experience what I experience through my relationship with you. Your mentorship, impartation, and patience, are the reasons this book exists. I love you both! (Khaira and Rafael too.lol)

To every Pastor that I've been privileged enough to serve in any capacity, *Bishop Jeff Poole, Bishop Clint Brown,*

Pastor Paula White, Apostle Dannie Williams, and Bishop Eddie Tomberlin; it was an HONOR to serve each of you. Thank you for trusting me to serve the vision that God has given you. I'm grateful for the teachings that I received that will carry me for the rest of my life.

To ***my chorus teacher, Theresa Alexander***, you will never know the impact that you have had on my life. The four years that I sat under your tutelage exposed me to a level of excellence that was foreign to me. Thank you for operating and leading with a Spirit of Excellence! You helped change my perception and mentality, as a result of that, excellence became my new standard! You're AWESOME!

To all of my family and friends, thank you for being who you are. I am surrounded by people that believe in and push me to be the best ME!

Last but not least to the woman that God made just for me, ***Jasmine*** your drive, passion, tenacity, and boldness pushes me to be a better man. You are the first person to laugh at me, (LOL) but you are the first person to encourage me and hold me accountable to what God has assigned me to do. God knew exactly who I needed. He must REALLY love me because I get to do life with you! I LOVE YOU!:)

CONTACT INFORMATION

To book **Author Montel Powers** for your next event, or Worship Leader training, or to request prayer, please feel free:

Write to us at:
116 Penny Lane
Warner Robins, Georgia 31088

Email Us:
bookings@montelpowers.com

Visit our Website:
www.montelpowers.com

Follow us on Social Media:
Facebook - www.facebook.com/montelpowers
Instagram – www.instagram.com/montelpowers
Twitter - @montelpowers
Blog – MpowerYoublog.com

Made in the USA
Charleston, SC
18 June 2015